Old Far SURVIVAL

Splendid

PUBLICATIONS

The
Old Fart's Guide to
SURVIVAL

Dawn Cawley

Splendid

PUBLICATIONS

The Old Fart's Guide to Survival

Copyright © 2016 Dawn Cawley

The right of Dawn Cawley to be identified as the Author of the work has been asserted in accordance with the Copyright, Designs and Patents Act 1988.

Unit 7,
Twin Bridges Business Park
South Croydon
Surrey CR2 6PL

www.splendidpublications.co.uk

British Library Cataloguing in Publication Data is available from The British Library.

ISBN 9781909109704

Commissioning Editor: Shoba Vazirani

Designed by Swerve Creative Design & Marketing Ltd.
www.swerve-creative.co.uk

Jacket illustration by Tim Reedy www.timreedy.com

Printed and bound in the United Kingdom by CPI Group (UK) Ltd, Croydon, CR0 4YY

Contents

ONE
Celebrate!

Perhaps you've just marked another birthday, or maybe it's that odd twinge that triggered it off...you're getting older... time to reflect and take stock.

Hang on! Time isn't so important any more. You can reflect and restock any time you jolly well like. Let's celebrate instead! You've got your bus pass and managed to dodge the obituary column all this time – although it's always wise to check! – so forget all about looking back. Instead, why not book that holiday you've been thinking about for years, buy that outfit you've had your eye on or make a reservation at that fancy new restaurant that everyone's been raving about? If you should pop your clogs meanwhile, you won't get upset about it, will you? It's party time. Go on, enjoy the sunshine, tomorrow it might rain.

By now you know the score, you're older and wiser. You've sussed everything out, and know when it pays to be old and helpless and when it's advantageous to show off your wisdom and knowledge. You know when it's best to keep your mouth shut, particularly when it comes to family, don't you? (Let's leave that open to discussion.)

So why isn't everything hunky-dory, or that

popular bed of roses?

Many of our generation are plagued by stress, which, of course, isn't restricted to those of a certain age. It's no good keeping worries bottled up; let anxiety go. It helps to find the right person and talk to them. It might be a trusted friend or perhaps you need to seek professional, unbiased help; someone who has time to listen. It's pointless popping into an optician when you want the car serviced. You're wasting your time and theirs. It's a question of finding the right person for the job.

Stress is not a good thing. It's better to be laid back instead of getting your bowels in an uproar. (More on bowels later. Bet you can't wait, but hopefully you can!)

If it's the past you are worried about, it's

unalterable. You might have regrets but what is done, is done. As you get older your viewpoint often changes. What might have offended you years ago is now no longer a big deal. The goal posts have widened, and so they should. Everything has moved on and we must too.

Perhaps you've lost a friend through a disagreement? What a shame, all those years of friendship wasted. It seemed important at the time, but looking back, was it? With a bit of luck, it's not too late to do something about it, and you might be able to get in touch. Maybe he or she has also been thinking of you and the good times you shared way back.

I recently got a lot of pleasure through a phone call. Having taken down the Christmas cards, I noticed a friend I hadn't seen for years had written down her phone number. On the spur of the moment I decided to give her a call. It was fantastic and we were on the phone for ages, catching up. She was pleased to hear from me, especially as it was unexpected and she wasn't feeling well at the time. This triggered off the desire to get in touch with several other Christmas card contacts. No doubt the next phone bill will be mega – but what the hell!

Humour

Humour is essential as you grow older. It's pretty darned important when you are young too. It can be found in most situations if you look for it. A good laugh is the best type of medicine. It's good to give those chuckle muscles a treat and it gives a glum looking face a cheap face lift into the bargain, so find a reason to laugh.

Humour is not easy to define and it has changed considerably both on television and radio. The canned laughter doesn't help either. On many occasions the 'audience' seem to be splitting their sides, while I am sitting po-faced, thinking, 'Is it me?'

Sometimes something strikes you as being funny at the most inappropriate time.

Years ago I was sitting in the choir stalls at a special Lifeboat Service, when the minister began his sermon with, "Men that go down to the sea in ships, and do their business in turmoiled waters."

Was I the only one whose fertile imagination conjured up an amazing picture?

Realisation

Realisation can play tricks on you.

Several of us went away on a weekend jolly. One guy, over eighty was given a room on the ground floor, with a walk–in shower. He argued that he was not disabled, despite the blue badge in the front of his car.

I had a similar experience on the bus when a crowd of teenagers boarded. One felt hot and suggested that he opened a window. His friend said, "Better ask the old lady sitting beside you."

I almost clobbered him with my handbag, until I realised that there were more of them than me. The sense of survival kicked in and I was keen to avoid the graveyard, so I buttoned my lip and quietly seethed. Only afterwards did

I realise that he was right. I am an old lady.

On retelling the story to my son I assured him that I was determined to grow old disgracefully, to which he replied, "Mother, you have!"

Complacency

Don't become complacent.

Just because you're a senior citizen there is no need to go around looking like Wurzel Gummage. You owe it to yourself to look presentable. Respect yourself. Make the most of what you've got, with a little help from your friends, ie the hairdresser, they're gold dust (there's a hairy section coming later), the dentist and those special toiletries and little facial aids that only women know about.

Beware of going out smelling of Vick or embrocation. (Also the revolting smell of fags

— phew!) and always look in the mirror, not the tiny one in the bathroom that shows the daub of toothpaste on one of the chins, or the lipstick on the teeth, and misses the full picture. A full length mirror is the answer. You can check your flies aren't undone, and turn around to check there is no bum cleavage or a skirt tucked seductively into your knickers. We've all seen it and done it. It usually happens when you go out feeling slightly gorgeous and you're completely unaware of the entertainment you are providing.

The days of burning the bra are over. Does size matter? Well, yes it does, at least in this context, with the wide (did I say wide?) range of fittings, B–K cups. The A cup now seems to be out of fashion, like virginity.

The problem is getting the right size and doing

the damn thing up, or undoing it, whichever the case. Men don't seem to have the same problem when it comes to underpants sizes.

My daughter bought a pack of underpants for me to give my son–in–law for Christmas. When wrapping them up in jaunty Christmas paper, I scribbled a friendly little note on the packaging, "Happy Christmas, Rog. Looking forward to seeing you in them!"

Unfortunately she had picked up the wrong size. It was her mistake, so I was determined she would be the one to face the supervisor in M&S and explain.

I digress, so let's return to the Men's Department…Many seem to opt for the high waist band. Perhaps they relish the added warmth around the waist and under the armpits.

Women benefit from an elasticated waist. What a fantastic invention! Those extra inches can be hidden beneath a baggy t–shirt, a warm sweater or even a neat twin set worn over a skirt or trousers.

Dress for your age. We've laughed at the old guy, shirt unbuttoned to the waist, sporting a dangler, and the old gal displaying knobbly knees, scraggy neck and scrawny arms. It's better covered up, for it doesn't do a lot for the image.

Here's a thought…
Once you're in Heaven, do you get stuck wearing the clothes you were buried in, for eternity?

Pay attention to those cracks and crevices lurking beneath body hangovers. Water and sweat can hang around there, and become red, raw and mighty painful. Dry carefully after a bath or shower, and pat with a piece of toilet paper to absorb the moisture.

Loss of elasticity (I'm not talking about the waist band) and the pull of gravity manifests itself with age, not only externally, but internally. Just because the main building has been removed, don't take it for granted that the scaffolding has gone.

Let's get back to the external. Unless you have a personal Gok Wan, (I wish I had) or you possess a purse the sized of Sharon Osborne's, it's your fate to learn to live with that pull of gravity.

Try to ignore the stomach getting in the way when you have a toe-nail cutting session, and forget melons and cucumbers and think of exercise.

***

Well, that's enough thinking!

Kidding apart, we know fresh air and walking is not only good for us, but it is enjoyable. It takes us out and about and it's a great idea to include in our daily routine.

Perhaps this is your opinion on diet and weight: 'At our age, why bother? As long as it isn't a health issue, why worry?'

However, you've got to admit that the odd ounce can turn into a pound. Then it furtively increases into a stone. Suddenly you realise that you are lugging around a fat suit and look like a

Michelin man.

Many of us are either too thin, or too chubby (is chubby another way of saying fat?) I fall into this category.

If God had wanted us to touch our toes, He'd have put them on our knees.

TWO
Move

Exercise

Sorry, but I had to sneak it in somewhere, and this is where the sense of humour has to come in. We know how important it is to keep mobile, but, to be honest, jogging all over the place in trainers, running x number of miles per day, clad in shorts, t-shirt and a sweat incrusted head band, isn't everybody's scene.

What can be done?

Don't panic, Mainwaring! Get off that jogging machine and don't embark on a violent diet. Be sensible. Eating hardly anything and exercising like a maniac could land you in big trouble. You could initially lose weight and feel chuffed as a result, but it won't last. As soon as you try to eat normally, it all piles back on. It has to be done gradually and sensibly. Also your resistance will drop and you open the door to every type of bug doing the rounds.

If going to the gym, or keep fit classes have always been your lifestyle – good on you! If not, and you decide to give it a whirl, then be careful or you could end up with a coronary. It might be safer working up a sweat with a curry.

Why not try toning up with an exercise DVD, your choice of level, in the privacy of your own home? That, to my mind, is a much better option. You can switch it off when you've had enough and you won't have to rely on a Good Samaritan to bring you home or take you to hospital afterwards.

Cut down on those 'naughty but nice' treats. Up the fruit and veg and cut down on the portion sizes. Think before putting that packet of biscuits into your wire basket – you don't really need them, do you? And take a squint at the calorie chart on that ready-made meal.

Save a treat for a special occasion. Healthy eating equals a healthy body.

Adjust your life style according to your age and fitness, but remember a pint in each hand does not qualify as weight lifting, and … beware…not too many glasses of vino!

If you're not up to it, take a buggy on to the golf course instead of trudging around knowing you'll suffer the next day. It might save you a week in bed with a dodgy back.

Here's a thought…
Why is it that we've got Body Shops everywhere, yet that is the very thing they don't sell!

Sport and games

The grandchildren are always keen for you to join in their games of football or rounders. Watch it, for it could lead to a broken leg or arm, which could cause you a lot of pain, discomfort and many repercussions. Be wise before the event and know your limits.

On the other hand, if you are A okay and up for it, go ahead, have a swing or a turn on the trampoline, you know you want to, and the kids will love you for it.

Don't be too exuberant and land in next-door's pond. The children might find it embarrassing having to knock on a neighbour's door with the plea, 'please can we have our granny/grandad back?'

It doesn't snow often, but one of my ancient friends decided to go sleighing with his grandchildren. He hasn't been the same since – the old back, y'know. Mind you, his chiropractor's doing very nicely out of it!

Pitfalls

There's no need to spell this out. It's apparent with every twinge, every glance in an unsympathetic mirror, not to mention those minor irritations, (what about that itchy back?), deterioration of sight, hearing and forgetfulness. What did I say?

How often have you made out a shopping list and left it behind, or gone upstairs and wondered what the devil for? One of my favourite tricks is taking a few letters to post, putting them in a prominent position in the front of the car. I usually return home complete with letters still in the car.

Why is it some mornings we wake up feeling like last Friday's fish 'n chips? We're all in the same boat. It happens! Let's face it – we're slowing down.

TWO Move

Many years ago my husband and several of his retired male friends formed a walking group called The Walkie Talkies. They would meet on alternate Thursday mornings and follow a route prepared by one of the members, ending up for lunch at a convenient hostelry.

When he became ill and couldn't manage the walk, I drove him direct to the meal, where, for an hour or two, he would enjoy the company, until one of them brought him home.

The group is still going strong (although, perhaps 'strong' might not be the appropriate word any more). It's a smaller group now and the length of the walk has shortened considerably, and I guess it's more talkies instead of walkies. It's a good compromise and long may it last.

We should be grateful for any aids and give

praise where praise is due. Bless those specs and hearing aids (that's when you can find them) and the hip replacements and the removal of cataracts.

Pensioners' perks

Apart from the bus pass there are loads of other concessions. Look no further than the theatre, cinema or those tempting deals at so many restaurants.

I've no shame in flashing my senior citizen's card if it gets me a cheap meal Mon–Fri, or a few bob off a tin of paint or a roll of wallpaper. Watch out for those special deals on a Tues.

Out of season holidays are fabulous. They are cheaper and can be great fun. There's a 'holiday special' and suggestions about what to take, further on in this book. Mind you, if you are on your own there is generally a hefty single supplement.

Occasionally Saga offer a no single supplement on some of their river cruises, but it don't come cheap. Congrats for this, Saga, keep up the good work. I think things are slowly improving but please, let's have reductions on more holidays soon.

My gripe is to the majority of travel agents. Isn't it about time they did something to please everyone?

I can understand why parents object when they see how the price rockets during the school holidays. I'm sure I did a moan when it affected our family, but I'm happy for them to fight their own battle now.

Never turn down an offer of help, either in the house or in the garden. Tell 'em it's appreciated and provide a cup of tea and their favourite biscuit and they'll be pleased to help again. Value contributions.

Here's a thought...
Give 'em a snack and they'll come back.

THREE
Get it right

Misunderstanding

This can be caused through hearing incorrectly and 'getting the wrong end of the stick.'

It's a good idea to make note in a diary/calendar, or both, of the time and place you have arranged to meet a friend. Maybe the correct entrance might help.

I've been known to wait outside M&S, looking at my watch and fuming, while a friend has been doing exactly the same thing – at the other end!

Selecting the wrong word is common and often hilarious, but perhaps that's merely a pigment of the imagination!

I was somewhat concerned when a friend mentioned that she was a great believer in euthanasia, and she was going home to take a pill, as she found it warded off the common cold. Indeed it would, but I'll stick with Echinacea, and, incidentally, incompetent and incontinence can add a whole new edge to any story.

Mistaken identity

Can you put a name to a face? I can't and I'm not alone. Faces become familiar in various venues and settings. It might start with a nod or a smile and then the exchange of a few words, maybe at the bus stop or in the street.

This happened in Sainsbury's a while ago. One of my cronies was shopping, and saw the usual fellow stacking the shelves. They exchanged the usual, *"hello"* and then the stacker's face suddenly clouded over as he imparted the sad news, *"Ron died, y'know."*

"I'm sorry to hear that," was my friend's reply. He's still puzzling over who poor departed Ron was.

Many years ago, when I was working in a baby clinic, covering for holiday leave, one of the nurses came in.

"Dawn!" she exclaimed, *"How lovely to see you."* I hadn't a clue who it was, but hoped I'd get

the message. We covered practically every subject; family, holidays, hobbies etc, until eventually she said, *"Weren't we devils at school."*

At last enlightenment clicked. It was like the sun appearing from behind a cloud.

"Yes, weren't we, Ann," I replied triumphantly.

Simple appliances

I'm calling these 'simple,' as opposed to the technical comments later.

Most of us have got to grips with the TV, although a few of us are still not one hundred per cent happy when it comes to recording, and it's confusing with the variety of buttons and gadgetry inviting you to press. I've come to terms with changing channels, but when it's a choice of checking the weather, I much prefer waiting until our local bloke comes on after the news. It's easier than having to get someone in to reprogramme the entire works?

On occasions I've been perched in front of the TV, when the phone has rung. I grab the nearest item, only to discover I've got the remote pressed against my ear. By the time I've located the right instrument, the answer machine has cut in.

Some people adapt to new appliances easily. They whiz around on their 'snail,' taking photos on their mobile phone, check the racing results on an iPad, and are completely computer literate. How I wish I was!

I don't suppose they have any problem with those high toilet seats either. If I managed to get on board, I reckon I'd have to stay there, legs dangling, until someone helped me off.

Pleasantries

Wear a smile.

It poses many questions. Is he or she gaga? They've always got a stupid smile on their face and folk wonder what they've been up to. Keep them guessing!

A smile always makes you appear ..... interesting.

When meeting anyone, after the usual greeting, be careful. "*How are you?*" can open a can of worms. You'll probably get a detailed account of the last visit to the surgery or hospital and a full blown description of bowel movements. (How easy it is to get involved in this.) Not to mention Uncle Fred's dicky ticker and Aunt Mabel's ulcer and every conceivable ailment under the sun.

Here's a thought…
What disease did cured ham actually have?

Watch out for 'alternative medicine,' that's another trap. You could end up in a similar situation. Everyone has their favourite illness and can usually recommend a cure.

The Doctor *"don't know nuffin,"* and he, of course, is frequently up for discussion and often pulverization. He's either God's gift, or a complete waste of space. There's no pleasing everyone.

The world is full of hypochondriacs. Not only do they have a seat marked RESERVED in the surgery, but they look up details in a book, or better still go 'on line' for their diagnoses. Prescriptions are looked up on Google and they can reel the names off as effectively as Alan Titchmarsh gets his tongue around hippeastrum.

FOUR
Looking your best

Hair

Finding a good hairdresser is like winning the lottery.

If you are fortunate enough to have your own hair, by now you've proved it has a will of its own. Maybe you fall into a category where, if you were a tyre, you'd be declared 'illegal'. This would be no big problem, at least, not for the male species.

A Phil Mitchell is all the rage. It's tidy and cheap to maintain and you'll be the envy of the younger generation who pay a considerable amount of money for that particular style.

A good hairdresser is an expert. They can dabble with the colour, comb a few strands of hair over a bald spot, tease a handful of curls seductively over the forehead to hide the wrinkles, then lacquer everything in place so that you look fantastic. When you leave the salon you feel uplifted and a whole lot better for the visit.

If you fancy a bit of titivation at home, don't mix up the lacquer with the deodorant. It's easily done. A hurried squirt under the armpits could prove disastrous!

Treat the mirror as a friend, even though it can cause you embarrassment. Why hadn't I seen that three-inch hair curling beneath the chin? Did they notice it yesterday at the coffee morning? How long has it been there?

As you get older, rogue hair can manifest itself in a variety of places. There could be a toothbrush effect or a single straggler in the ears or nostrils.

Life can be unfair. A follicle-challenged head can often produce a chest like a forest or Dennis Healey eyebrows.

Idiosyncrasies
(I've just learnt how to spell it!)

We've all got them and it's not a bad thing. It's our little speciality.

Maybe we enjoy a leisurely look at the paper, probably over breakfast. We've got the time, why not? The crossword appeals to many and it keeps the brain active, although you might be unpopular if you take it (the crossword, not the brain) into the loo while others are waiting outside breaking their necks!

Have you a weather complex? Don't let it spoil your day and stay indoors if there is a threat of rain. On the other hand, it's useful to know whether (no pun intended) you should take an umbrella or a sunhat.

How many of us nod off in front of the telly? It's galling when you've slept through the unveiling of 'who done it'. Stick the recorder on – just in case. It's easily deleted afterwards. No need to let on to the family!

Give yourself something to look forward to at the end of the day. A little treat: you've earned it. What's wrong with a glass or two of sherry or wine? Whatever tickles the palate. When bedtime beckons, perhaps you'd enjoy a nice warm bath. Use the essence you were given for Christmas, or are you saving it for a raffle. You could even take your drink into the bathroom; it might taste even better there.

The luxury of a comfortable bed with an electric blanket or a hot water bottle becomes more appealing as you grow older, especially in the winter, so no excuse for staying up late. That happens anyway.

Wallow in the book you are reading. Enjoy the time spent listening to *The Archers*, you're allowed to. Choose your own particular entertainment and add it to your life whenever you have the chance.

Why not break the rules now and again,

change the routine, swap or reverse the activities. Grab time for yourself. Have an aim – a goal.

Sometimes we bear grudges…they hurt me etc. Forget it. We've no time for that sort of thing. Sod 'em and move on. Everyone is here for a purpose, even those who are a pain in the bum.

It's far easier to complain than praise. Let's try and balance it up. When things please us, say so. The person responsible will appreciate a pat on the back or a favourable comment and it encourages them to keep up the high standard. Life is full of kicks in the backside.

Loneliness

Loneliness can take over your life if you let it, particularly if you live on your own.

Perhaps it's your choice and you want to shut

yourself away, preferring your own company and keeping away from other people.

Sometimes loneliness catches you unaware and it suddenly happens. You've had a lovely day with friends or family. You've enjoyed yourself and there has been plenty of fun and laughter. You wave goodbye, shut the door and that's it – silence. You feel melancholy. The day that you looked forward to for some time is over and, once again, you are by yourself.

Try not to become depressed. Plan a treat, maybe meeting a friend for a meal in town, or arrange a coach trip. Even a visit to the theatre or a film is cheering. Why not take a look in the address book and write to or phone a friend? They might also be feeling lonely and be delighted to hear from you.

Here's a thought…
If you've a radio, you've a friend. Feeling lonely, bored, or fed-up? Help is at hand – switch on!

Hopefully there are a few more suggestions further on that might prove helpful in preventing loneliness and there's a section on friends coming up.

No matter what our situation in life, from time to time we feel insecure, helpless and lonely. It's so much better if we can share our feelings. There are like–minded people around, so how about getting together, teaming up and enjoying a feeling of belonging. There are a variety of clubs and societies where you will be made welcome and it's an opportunity to make new friends. If you can't find anything that interests you, why not start a group of your own. You could call it The Old Farts Association, or just Old Fart Ass for short. Perhaps the initials might be effective, OFA. Friday night is OFA night has a certain ring to it.

When you meet new people you learn something different. Not necessarily a nugget of knowledge, but their attitude to life.

Voluntary work is a good way to become involved and there's plenty to choose from. Pick something you will enjoy. The library is the ideal place to look for info. If you take a new voluntary interest up, not only will you be getting out of the house, but you'll be contributing to something worthwhile. You'll feel part of it, and gain personal satisfaction. Loneliness will be a thing of the past.

Hobbies and interests

Select as many as you can but don't let anyone talk you into something that really isn't your scene. It's easily done. If your heart is set on learning a language, joining a flower arranging class is a waste of time.

How about joining a choir? Men are particularly welcome. A church choir might be the answer. There's always a lot going on connected with the church and they're always grateful for help. If you're not into singing then maybe Am Dram might be the answer. If you don't relish going on stage, people are needed behind the scenes; lighting, sound, prompting, or with the costumes and make-up.

Family commitments prevent some of us from having a hobby. Are you responsible for looking after the grandchildren? This can be both rewarding and tiring. Don't forget 'you ain't as young as you were.' Sorry, I shouldn't keep reminding you!

Grandchildren are a great joy and it's sometimes fun to lead them on – just a little bit. After a session with the grandchildren, the odd remark or turn of phrase that they have heard can come into their conversation when they return home.

The parents immediately say, "*You can always tell they've spent the day with Grandma.*" The voice of experience!

Of course, when they are young and you've had 'one of those days,' you can always resort to climbing into the playpen and giving them the run of the house!

Friends

Most of us have a variety of friends, eg those that you'd trust with your life and can rely on. (Diamonds.)

There are those that are fun to be with and you don't have to watch your P's and Q's (pure gold). Other friends you enjoy meeting, but you find you don't completely relax in their company. Maybe you have to be a tad careful over a topic of conversation. It could be that you don't know them well enough or haven't known them for long (gold plated). Perhaps in time they will move into the 'pure gold' category.

Everyone is different and often have their own trademark. Perhaps they are a trifle nosy or snobbish for your liking? It doesn't matter, for that's the way they are. It's part of the fun and no big deal. They are happy – that's great. We all have odd little quirks, which can be endearing or irritating, depending on our mood, so what? We're older, more laid back and can cope – can't we?

Remember that old radio programme years ago featuring Beryl Reid as a naughty schoolgirl? She spoke of another girl and described her as, *"My best friend, and I hate her."* Perhaps you have a friend who always looks fantastic, has an amazing house, brilliant children and can muster up a cordon bleu meal by the time you've removed your plastic rain hat.

Share your embarrassment with others. Give a slight raise of the eyebrow or a wink and you'll get away with anything, providing they've a sense of humour. If they haven't – too bad.

Picture a crowded waiting room, or a restaurant. You have a deaf friend. They don't realise they are shouting and go into intimate detail about their prostate examination, or the sex life of a cousin. How embarrassing is that? Some folk like to share an opinion, which can be hilarious. A while ago, at an opera, the heroine, who possessed a lovely voice, but was lacking in the acting department, unconvincingly sang, "*It is Don Jose and he has a gun.*"

A senior citizen yelled out, "*For God's sake shoot her, then we can all go home.*"

This brought more applause than the singer.

FIVE
Getting away

Holidays

This is a huge topic of conversation, almost as common as discussing the weather, which is pretty important when selecting a holiday. What suits one person probably won't suit another. If a couple choose a holiday it should help if they have similar interests.

Family holidays can be expensive when the children are of school age. It's high season and the travel agent bangs up the price as soon as school breaks up. (I've been into all this.)

When you are single, make sure the person with whom you are travelling, is in agreement with your plans, especially if you are sharing a room. Single supplements are a killer, so it pays to share, but remember, it's a bonus if you can remain friends when you return home, so think carefully about this.

One of the perks of being a senior citizen is that we can go out of season, which is a bonus. It's cheaper, not so crowded and those on holiday are of a similar age group. Also, let's face it, although you love the kids, bless 'em, it's much more peaceful.

Some people choose a holiday where they can visit as many places as possible, while others prefer a more relaxing time. Everything is catered for nowadays from cruises to adventure holidays. It all depends on taste and finance. The choice is yours.

Although it's time consuming, part of the fun is going through brochures and deciding where to go. Read the small print carefully as it can add up to a lot more than you first anticipated with those hidden extras.

Most places have entertainment laid on, from bingo and dancing to shows. If you are a people watcher, there is entertainment in bucketfuls. Look no further than the people sitting nearby who eat in silence, loading up fork after fork of 'today's special'. As they're not talking it's generally a safe bet to assume they are married.

For extra entertainment, look to the dance floor. 'Movement,' is the operative word. There is always someone fatter/slimmer, older/younger, less/more mobile than yourself. You can see the expert and also a couple where the man is reluctant to take to the floor.

He's been badgered into it by a forceful, flamboyant, enthusiastic spouse, who will cut off his genitalia unless he obeys. While she is giving it socks, he is content to remain po-faced, hands hanging loosely by his side as he begrudgingly transfers his weight from one foot to the other. Happy holiday!

Why not give a dance display to embarrass the grandchildren? They'll be the only ones who care a jot. Everyone else is glad to see you're having a good time. Nobody stands out in a crowd and it doesn't matter if they do. The floor is peppered with Beryl Cook characters.

A team, young, honed and nubile, is generally responsible for the entertainment. They're in charge of the kids' club, sport programme such as table–tennis, archery etc and often take part in the evening entertainment, singing and dancing, full of energy and stamina. Many are excellent and of a very high standard, capable of giving *Strictly* a run for its money! They work hard and there is a great deal of talent out there.

Musical entertainment will include a vocalist. Maybe it's a man pensioned off from a cruise ship, who thinks he's Frank Sinatra, or a well endowed woman with an economical shirt and a low cut neckline who bounces around the stage like a beach ball. The men are mesmerised wondering if the performer and outfit might part company.

Whatever the entertainment, there's something for everyone and you're on holiday so just enjoy it!

Holiday reading

At last you've the opportunity to get your teeth into a good book, or perhaps not such a good book. Anyhow, it's one you've been planning to read for a long time. It might be Shakespeare, *The Development of Tea Throughout The Ages*, or a hot novel by Jackie Collins.

Better still the third book in the series of *Fifty Shades*. (If you've survived the first two.) It will cause a reaction after a few pages, *"Blimey, it was never like that for me."* Then reality sets in, get real – it's fiction for goodness sake! The next stage is analysing the positions and working out if it is humanly possible. Some couples might decide to experiment for themselves and end up in A and E, which would take some explaining!

Less obvious travel essentials

Toilet roll

Wet Wipes

Pantie Liners

Emodium

Ex–lax

Eye drops

Athlete's foot cream and powder

Hearing aid batteries

Denture repair kit

Band aid

Support bandage
Super glue
Stain remover
Viagra
Lubricant
Vick vapour rubs
Ointment (It's difficult to explain in a foreign country that you require something for piles.)

Here's a thought…
Why do they call it an asteroid when it's outside the hemisphere, but call it a haemorrhoid when it's in the butt?

FIVE *Getting away*

Super glue is important. One fellow lost a lens down the toilet. Fortunately he didn't throttle his wife when she made an announcement during the evening meal, "*Can't think why he was wearing glasses. He only needs them for magnification. Haw! haw!*"

There was uproar in a hotel room in Cyprus. Shortly after arrival, a couple were aware of an undetected low humming sound in their room. A member of staff was summoned to investigate. He checked the wires, plugs, and moved all the furniture, only to discover a spare hearing aid in a case had become activated.

On another occasion a friend of mine screamed when she saw a huge insect of the cockroach variety lurking in the shower. With the first drip of water the creature hastily disappeared through a gap behind a pipe. I mentioned that I hoped it wouldn't find its way into my room, which was next door.

A couple of days later at 5.45am I ventured into the bathroom for a call of nature. On return in the half–light I saw a long, black object by the wardrobe. My heart was pounding and the brain (what little there is of it) went into overdrive. I grabbed a glass and placed it over the uninvited guest, only to discover in the morning that I had captured a doorstop.

Experiences

We are all here for a purpose.

As we grow older we have more idea how to handle situations. If you saw someone in the street who recently lost a dear one, it would have been tempting to avoid them, for you're not sure what to say, but now you realise that they will appreciate a friendly, *"Hullo, how are you doing?"*

Never say you know how they are feeling unless you are in the same situation. Only those who have been there truly know.

Make someone feel special by giving them your full attention. Never judge: accept. You might be able to help. (NB help, not interfere.)

There is generally another point of view. Listen and try to understand. Circumstances alter decisions and views, and others don't always act the way you expect or hope.

Don't hold back from someone close, be there for them. You can't expect love if you're not prepared to give it. Everyone feels so much better if they know someone cares. With age you can often tell when a person needs to talk, or wants a bit of help. We can decide how to respond and focus on their need.

Share fears, for it's not a weakness, others have them too. Soul bare, share problems, but select the right person. They might be able to offer a solution.

There is a first time for everything. We all make mistakes but people will respect you far more if you admit them. Accept our own and other people's imperfections. We've all got them. Everyone has regrets, but try to forget them and move forward.

Maybe we heard something that we don't want to hear, possibly criticism. Can we take it? How will we react? Show maturity, perhaps the criticism is justified. Think about it before reacting. How we react is our choice.

Licenced to drive

Wow! That's a tricky one.

We're not all drivers, but if you are, there might be a time in your life when you have to consider if you should be on the road.

My ex–next door neighbour (who has now moved to Nottingham to be closer to her family) suddenly made the decision to pack up driving. She no longer felt happy behind the wheel, and decided that instead of the expense of running a car, she would put the money towards taxis, or make greater use of her bus pass. Being a game old bird, she walked to the shops, lost weight and became fit. That's great, providing the old legs are up to it!

If you are disabled, or movement is limited and you are becoming a danger, it's not so straightforward. Who will have the courage to tell you and will you accept it?

My son and daughter have admitted that they have discussed this difficult situation and I hope they won't have to face it for a very long time. At the moment it's still at the roll of the dice stage.

It's wonderful to have the independence of a car, but frightening when you could be hurt or, worse still, fatally injure someone else.

Rosemary, (not her real name) who is a tad older than me and a sociable animal, is generous in offering lifts, and insists on taking her turn. It's not always possible to think of an excuse not to accept, and usually ends up with yours truly in the front, a whiter shade of pale, while the others sit in the back, quietly praying.

One of the group suggested that I 'have a word.' My response was, no way, it's up to the family to tell her.

Here's another thought...
Change is inevitable, except from a vending machine.

We're forever making progress, meeting new people, making commitments, changing attitudes and building new dreams. We know that there can be more than one answer to a question and both can be right. Life is too short for an issue and it isn't worth it. Believe in yourself and look to the moment. Encourage yourself and others. Offer comfort and receive it. We're not here by chance.

Perhaps you are hiding behind a mask because of vulnerability or for protection. Is it time to drop that mask?

Have you ever drawn the short straw and found that you have been lumbered with something you don't want to do? It happens! It doesn't always turn out to be the pain in the backside you anticipated. Perhaps you had to meet someone whom you thought you had nothing in common with; different generation, background and interests. It could turn into a pleasant surprise with both gaining new knowledge and mutual enjoyment from one another. You could end up wanting to hear more and investigate further. Things often turn out better than anticipated.

Everyone feels better if they know somebody cares, so why not give a friend a gentle touch on the arm or a hug?

Life is full of suffering and celebration, pain and pleasure, and we all play a part.

SIX
Watch out

Accidents

Think before you do anything stupid like venturing out when it's icy. Don't be rash. A nasty fall might 'cook your goose,' landing you in trouble and causing a lot of extra work for friends and relations.

Throw on a coat when it is cold outside, even if it's only to bring in the washing.

Banisters are there for a purpose. Catch hold

of the perishers – that's what they're there for!
Try not to lose your balance, especially when
you've both legs in one knicker. You might fall
over and clobber your head on something lethal,
and watch out for the family pet, especially if
you've had a drink or two.

It usually happens quickly and unexpectedly.
Maybe your mind was on something else.

One morning, before dressing, I had a stupid
desire to rinse out a top. It was a fine day, which
inspired me to hang it on the clothes line. As
water cascaded from the garment, I managed to
slip and measured my length on the concrete. It
was not a pretty sight, blood mingled with water
as I crept indoors. I sneaked into the bathroom
to patch things up and realised what a plonker I
was, and how much worse it could have been.

Tolerance

Allowances have to be made frequently.

Maybe you're not deliberately hogging the loo. It's a slow motion day when things take longer than expected and as a result practically all the toilet roll has been used.

For goodness sake, make sure there is a replacement as soon as possible, otherwise you could be in deeper trouble, as would the next person!

Various foods can cause problems and as a result unpleasant smells assail the nostrils. An expression comes to mind which sums up the situation (although that expression is not completely accurate) 'sitting close to the wind.' Being unprepared, a spray is never to hand. The same problem can be worse at night when the duvet floats. Christmas is particularly a bad time. Blame those sprouts, or get a dog.

Love

Love is a four-lettered word along with lust and all the rest! There can be confusion between the two, but believe me, they are very different and it's wise to keep your head screwed on. (No joke intended – well, not really.)

Love is complex. There are many types of love. There is family love, which includes brothers, sisters, sons, daughters, parents, cousins and friends, then of course, there is the love that we read about and watch on television and see in the theatre or at the cinema.

Most important of all is the love that we feel

in a close, personal relationship. It is possible to love more than one person, but probably in a different way.

The definition of love in my dictionary (ancient though it may be) describes it as … warm affection, sexual passion. Lust, on the other hand, is described as …strong desire for sexual gratification. Both words mention sexual, and that's probably where so many of the youngsters slip up, so to speak!

Hopefully we older folk have 'wised up'. Passion is a strongly felt desire. It is an emotion, but not necessarily sexual. You might have a passion for music or sport.

Emotion is when you are greatly moved almost to bursting point. There may be tears, excitement, pleasure, jealousy, grief and, of course, love.

Golden oldies have grown old together. They are happy and content and have known each other inside out for years. But not everyone is as fortunate. Maybe they have never married, or, because of death or divorce, they find themselves single again.

New relationships can blossom, often unexpectedly. Honesty is vitally important. What are they both looking for? Are they looking for the same thing? Is one of them capable of a physical relationship devoid of emotion or love?

Make sure each one of you is singing off the same hymn sheet otherwise someone will get hurt.

It's much easier nowadays if you are seeking a partner. There are dating agencies, many of them online, and of course, there are ads in newspapers and in magazines, (not forgetting 'helpful' friends).

There's a pretty good record with dating agencies. Those that join are eager to meet a compatible partner, possibly leading to romance, and, maybe, marriage. (Beware jokers.)

It's an opportunity to be selective, as the details are there for all to see, just read the blurb… 'Single, four grown up children, one in Pentonville. Owns two dogs and a pet tarantula named Ethel.' If that's what floats your boat, what are you waiting for?

Friends can take a hand in match making.

A while ago one of my school friends was recovering from the death of her husband. Neighbours, being sympathetic, invited her out to a restaurant for a meal. They also invited a divorced male friend.

The evening was a disaster! It turned out that the two 'guests' had been married previously – to each other.

How often does a person tick all the boxes? There is no perfect man or woman.

A woman might enjoy a spot of romance, the unexpected compliment, a bunch of flowers or some little love gesture, whereas a man is content with a peaceful, comfortable existence with no hassle. It's good if you can be content with what you can tick and overlook the rest.

Never assume anything, and don't take

anything for granted. Appearances can be deceptive. The little old man with a long white beard toddling along on his Zimmer may have a fire in the cellar, whereas a Peter Pan look alike may find that there is no spark left in his Bunsen burner, and his self-raising power has passed its sell by date.

It's a waste of time trying to impress by saying that you are 'on the pill.' Everyone knows it's no longer a form of birth control, merely a medication for blood pressure.

If sex is on the agenda, the moans and groans could be due to cramp or sciatica, not ecstasy.

Chemistry is impossible to describe and I won't attempt it. It's magical and special and doesn't often happen, but if it does, oh boy, will you know it!

On the pull

It's never too late y'know, and if that's your aim, good luck to you, but always be subtle, otherwise it can cause great hilarity to observers.

A few months ago a group of us went to a charity luncheon in town. We had an excellent meal followed by a raffle, and there were considerably more women than men.

Mrs X, a seventy–plus, twice divorced, available female considered it a hunting ground and was placed on our table next to the only unsuspecting male. This was her target for the day and she ordered a bottle of wine, which she hurriedly consumed while turning her attention in his direction.

The others sitting at the table watched in

fascination as, along with the wine, she poured out her life story, stopping frequently to pat his hand. Having established that he drove a BMW, she suggested a lift back to her luxury flat, with balcony.

Eventually the penny dropped, and the victim hastily excused himself, explaining that his parking meter had running out. Alas he failed to mention that he possessed a disabled badge and didn't need to pay. He hasn't attended the charity lunch since.

SEVEN
Keeping up
Modern Technology

You can either sink or swim, or maybe, like me, wallow in the murky depths or crawl under a convenient stone in the hope that someone in a shiny wet suit will come along and rescue you. Many of my bright friends have moved with the times. They possess computers, laptops, iPads etc, and know how to use them. Sadly I have only just mastered the electric toothbrush.

I watch in admiration as the grandchildren press icons and move things up and down, although I sometimes worry that their power of conversation might suffer.

A while ago my grandson invited me upstairs to "*take a look at my wii.*" I was relieved to discover that it was his latest piece of technical equipment.

One day I will find time to concentrate on the computer. It opens up a whole new world to both young and old and there is much to learn. Technology is incredible. It's progressing and improving all the time and has become a fulfilling and necessary part of life. Don't be afraid of it – embrace the challenge.

Family

Family are vitally important. The younger generation are in the same situation that we were in years ago. We've been there, done that, and we should be able to gauge everything properly, but it's not as simple as that. Times have changed. We have single parents, and parents who both work full time, so how do you manage a happy balance?

Are you spending quality time with the family, or imposing? Is it the right time to have your say, or would it be better to keep your mouth shut? (Particularly where children are concerned.) It can be tricky.

The younger generation tend to make last minute arrangements, which can cause misunderstanding. Things need to be planned ahead.

Having kept dates free in the past and no invitation is forthcoming, you fill a slot, then at the last minute an invite arrives, and you are not available. It's not a question of what you prefer to do, it's more a feeling of filling a blank page while the grains of sand are still flowing freely through the egg timer.

It's difficult when you see young people making mistakes and there is nothing you can do about it. Just be there for them when they need help, and forget those words, "*I told you so*," and "*If only you'd listened to me*." They'll thank you in their heart for not saying them.

Age hits you in various ways. You might notice your children's hair turning grey, and it's

SEVEN *Keeping up*

not unusual to look in the mirror and see one of your parents looking back at you. On occasions you hear words being repeated to grandchildren that you have used to your children so long ago.

There's no place like home and you appreciate it and your independence more as you grow older, but sometimes for our own health and safety an alternative is necessary.

We still need to feel in control of our life and we feel resentful if decisions are made on our behalf and without our agreement. It isn't always easy to come up with something that suits everyone. Circumstances vary and often choices are limited or unavailable. What might suit one person might be totally unacceptable to another and many people are not prepared to see another point of view. A medical problem might decide where you go either temporarily or on a permanent basis, but long–term residence should never be forced on anyone of a sound mind without their agreement.

Horror stories are heard frequently and conditions must improve so that every residential home is of the highest standard they can possibly be.

Care in the community has become popular and it can work well as it allows an elderly person to remain in their own home. Often it is a relation or family friend and they become important and can be relied upon.

Sadly this is not always the case and a variety of carers come into the home, which doesn't always help the continuity. The carer has many homes to visit and time is limited.

Perhaps he/she is in a rush to get to the next visit and corners are cut and there is not enough time to build a relationship. More recruitment is needed for trustworthy, available carers.

I have a couple of friends who live in sheltered accommodation. They are very happy as there is plenty going on and they have made many new friends. One of them even has a resident 'toy boy' (as she calls him). I think he is only a couple of years younger than her – they're both over eighty in any case!

Moving in with family can work providing every member concerned is one hundred per cent in favour. (Especially if it's in–laws.) On all sides there must be responsibility and respect. Everyone has to have their own space and they need ground rules, including finance, chores and privacy and, of course, who is in charge of the remote control!

An elderly person moving in with a son or daughter must understand that they no longer rule the roost or make household decisions. It no longer about them and they can't expect teenage children to be quiet.

There also has to be consideration on behalf of the younger generation. If they agree to opening their home to a parent, they have to appreciate that the person involved has been used to living in their own home and there is the need to be tolerant and accommodating.

Don't be selfish and expect all the attention. It's about sharing. If there is likely to be a clash of personalities – forget it. Explore other possibilities.

SEVEN *Keeping up*

Feuds

Family feuds can go on for generations. Sometimes they've been going on for so long nobody can remember what caused them in the first place. All that aggro isn't worth it, you only become bitter.

There is still time to change things, to make things better, so don't faff around. Remarriage between oldies can cause a feud, particularly if there is baggage, ie children, which is so often the case. There can be resentment and complications from both sides with everyone asking the question: how am I affected?

An issue that's usually the first to rear its head is inheritance. What will the 'old dears' do with their dosh? Sex also might get a mention, and, of course, if old people still do it, "*It's disgusting*."

The oldies must be sensible and immediately update their will. Everything has to be fair and square and their wishes written in black and white.

This is extremely important. It must be thought through carefully and, if possible, discussed way before anyone pops their clogs. How many times has there been a big family fall out over a will? Get it sorted. As for that marriage document, it would be easier to forget it, and do what you like without the conflict.

When I'm not around I'd hate to think my family will disintegrate after my demise so I've sorted everything out to avoid any misunderstandings and quarrels.

After Christmas an elderly lady had a buffet meal for her three children and their families. Being very deaf, a member of the family phoned a few days later, mentioning that she hoped she hadn't felt isolated. The lady replied that she'd had a super time. She was delighted to see all the family happy and laughing together, enjoying each other's company, and she knew that it would be the same when she was no longer with them.

It's a lovely thought and I share the same optimism.

Finale

So there you have it – the seven phases of gran!

We are the lucky ones. Whatever lies ahead in the future can be turned into an adventure, a challenge. We old farts can have our say. We can stand up (possibly with the aid of a walking stick) and be counted. We can make a difference. Never underestimate an old fart. We're allowed to wear that t-shirt with pride.

You can't choose how you are going to die, but you can choose how you're going to live. What are we waiting for?

****

Also available from Splendid Publications

**Happily Ever After...? An Essential Guide
To Successful Relationships**
By Janet Clegg and Hilary Browne-Wilkinson

Congratulations, you've fallen in love and
from now on shouldn't it be 'happily ever
after?' Sorry, falling in the love is the easy bit!
With all the stresses and strains of modern
life it's becoming increasingly difficult to
sustain happy and loving relationships. In
the UK alone nearly half of all marriages
end in divorce and countless long-term
partnerships fail every day.

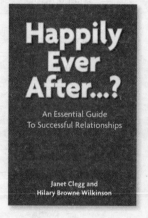

In Happily Ever After...? former London
divorce lawyers, Janet Clegg and Hilary
Browne Wilkinson, set out the vital
relationship questions we should all be asking ourselves to stop us falling into
the common traps which can derail even the most loving of couples.

So, if you've found the love of your life and are about to embark on a long-term
relationship, or even if you've been married or in a partnership for years, this no-
nonsense practical handbook, packed with easy to follow advice and examples,
can help you to look forward to a happier and loving future together.

£7.99 (paperback)

Daniel, My Son - A Father's Powerful Account Of His Son's Cancer Journey
By David Thomas

Daniel was just 17, rich of talent and full of dreams, when he received the devastating news that he had bone cancer all over his body. In pain and facing horrific treatment, his chances were slim. But Daniel refused to give up on life and studied Classics at Oxford, played with the BBC Symphony Orchestra, line-judged at Wimbledon and was chosen to carry the Olympic Torch. Meanwhile his heartbroken parents scoured the world for a cure and learnt to navigate the medical maze. Their mission was to create hope – for Daniel, themselves and all those facing the same nightmare: a child with cancer. This is a father's powerful story of his love for his son and humankind's overriding need for hope.

£7.99 (paperback)

**William and Kate's Britain -
An Insider's Guide to the haunts of the
Duke and Duchess of Cambridge**
By Claudia Joseph

Britain is an island with a rich cultural
heritage, which dates back to the Roman
era: it is a land of pubs and football; rock
music and opera; historic palaces and
village churches; breath-taking scenery
and ancient monuments. That's not to
mention its spectacular pageantry – the
royal wedding ceremony at St Paul's
Cathedral and the Queen's Diamond
Jubilee celebrations were beamed to
billions around the world. Now, in a
unique guide to the British Isles, royal
author Claudia Joseph goes behind the
scenes – and reveals the secrets – of
William and Kate's Britain.

£9.99 (paperback)

Order online at:
www.splendidpublications.co.uk